ROBERT CUMMING

JUST LOOK...
A Book about Paintings

CHARLES SCRIBNER'S SONS
New York

Introduction

This is a book about pictures and painting. I am going to show you some of the many different ways artists make pictures, and how they help us share their ways of looking.

Almost everything that is talked about in the book comes out of the pictures. So as well as reading the words, you will need to look very carefully at the pictures. As we go along, you will find quite a number of questions. Some will be easy, some more difficult, but the answers to almost all of them can be found in the pictures. What you need to do is just look.

The two pictures here show great Spanish artists at work. The man with the moustache is Diego Velasquez, who lived over 300 years ago. He is shown at work painting in one of his own pictures. The bald man is Pablo Picasso, who died in 1973. The photograph is from a film about him. If you turn to pages 21 and 37, you will be able to see what their paintings are like.

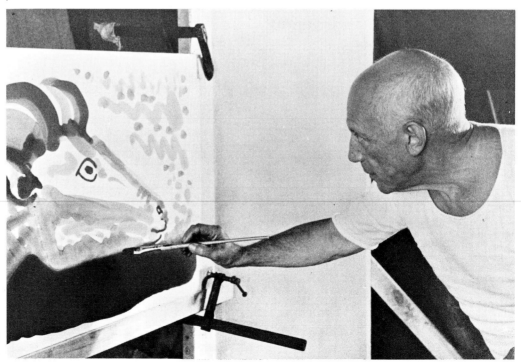

Pablo Picasso in the act of painting from the film *Le Mystère Picasso* (1956).

Diego Rodriguez de Silva Velasquez
(1599–1660)
SELF PORTRAIT (detail from
LAS MENIÑAS, 1656)
318 × 276cm
Museo Prado, Madrid

These two painters lived and worked in very different ways, but like all artists they looked hard and thought carefully about what they saw. I hope you will do the same.

JUST LOOK...

How many paintings do you think there are in this book?
Before you start to count, look very carefully at this famous
picture. It was painted by an Italian, Paolo Veronese, over
400 years ago, and it shows Jesus's first miracle, turning
water into wine at Cana. If you can find a magnifying glass,
you will be able to examine it very closely indeed.

Paolo Veronese (1526–1588)
THE MARRIAGE AT CANA (1563)
Musée du Louvre, Paris

Can you see any paint?
Can you see any brush marks?
Or do you only see colored dots?

You see, there are no actual paintings in this book, only printed reproductions. However good they may be, printed reproductions are always very different from the original paintings.

You will probably have to guess at the answer to the next question. How big do you think the original painting by Veronese is? Is it the same size as it is here? As big as a newspaper? As big as the wall of your room? Or as big as the side of a house?

Veronese's painting is about 47 times wider than our reproduction. It is one of the largest paintings in the world, 990cm wide and 666cm high. Measure this out on the ground and you will have an idea of just how big it is. You should be able to work out the size of the people in the original painting. Are they larger or smaller than real people?

The next picture is probably the most famous there is. It is Leonardo da Vinci's portrait of Mona Lisa, which is usually just called "The Mona Lisa". This is rather a small picture, only 53cm wide and 77cm high. It would fit into Veronese's enormous painting over 160 times.

You might think that since we cannot reproduce all the paintings in this book full size, at least we ought to make them all to the same scale. If we reproduced the Mona Lisa to the same scale as Veronese's picture, it would come out this size:

but then you would hardly be able to see Leonardo's painting at all.

So the printed reproductions in this book will all seem to be about the same size. Now that you know you are only looking at reproductions of paintings, I can talk about them as if they were the paintings themselves. Of course, this is cheating, and to see paintings in their full glory you should visit an art gallery. But whether you are looking at the actual paintings or at reproductions in a book, use your eyes and look.

Leonardo da Vinci (1452–1519)
MONA LISA (about 1503)
Musée du Louvre, Paris

The illustration on this page shows something you may never see, even in an art gallery. It is the back of a painting. The material is canvas, which has been pulled tight over a wooden frame called a stretcher. Most oil paintings are on this sort of canvas, which makes a firm, flat surface for the artist to paint on.

Sometimes there are labels or writing on the back of the painting. Like clues in a detective story, they can help us to learn what adventures the painting has been through. One of the labels has been enlarged so that you can read what it says.

In the course of hundreds of years, paintings may be bought and sold, even stolen. They may travel around the world, or survive wars and earthquakes. Sometimes they are cut up or painted over. Occasionally they have been attacked or ransomed. In a way, paintings are like people; each one has a life story. Like people, they become fragile as they get older and can easily be damaged. Paintings have to be looked after carefully if they are to have a long life.

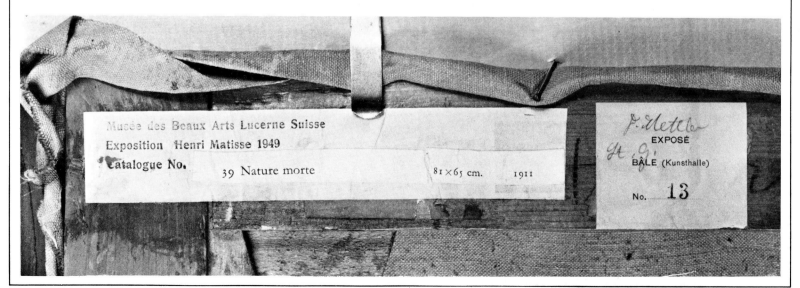

Musée des Beaux Arts Lucerne Suisse

Exposition Henri Matisse 1949

Catalogue No. 39 Nature morte 81×65 cm. 1911

EXPOSÉ

BÂLE (Kunsthalle)

No. 13

Now look at three very different pictures. The first was painted over 400 years ago by Pieter Breughel. It is like looking through a window at the cold, crisp, busy February day outside.

What do you think are the sizes of the paintings on these two pages? The answers are on page 59. You can find the sizes of the other paintings in this book in the captions. These are in small print beside the pictures and also tell you what gallery the originals are in, when the artist lived, and when the picture was painted.

Pieter Breughel (active 1551–died 1569)
FEBRUARY or THE GLOOMY DAY
(1565)
Kunsthistorisches Museum, Vienna

This painting isn't at all like a window. It comes out of the wall and is shaped rather like a box. This painting walks out of the wall into your room.

Why do you think it is called "Piano"? Is there anything about it that reminds you of the way a piano is made or the sound that one makes?

Richard Smith (1931–   )
PIANO (1963)
Tate Gallery, London

This painting was made with thick oil paint and bold brush strokes. You should be able to find every number from 0 to 9 in it. Here we have a picture that isn't like a window and doesn't come out of the wall at you. It stays in between and wants you to notice that it is flat on the wall so that you will see what is happening on its surface. This is a bit like looking at the palm of your hand. What you see is skin covered with lines and marks.

Jasper Johns (1930–   )
ZERO THROUGH NINE (1961)
Tate Gallery, London

Thomas Gainsborough (1728–1788)
MR AND MRS ANDREWS (about 1750)
70 × 119cm
National Gallery, London

Look at the pictures on these two pages.

Which are like windows you can see through?

Which come out of the wall at you?

Which are like looking at the palm of your hand?

Answers on page 59.

Claes Oldenburg (1929–   )
SOFT DRAINPIPE—BLUE
(COOL) VERSION (1967)
278 × 187 × 36cm
Tate Gallery, London

Jan Van Eyck (about 1390–1441)
THE MARRIAGE OF ARNOLFINI
(1434)
82 × 60cm
National Gallery, London

Kurt Schwitters (1887–1948)
PICTURE WITH LIGHT CENTRE (1919)
85 × 66cm
Museum of Modern Art, New York

What turns a flat piece of canvas into a window you can see through? These pages show three of the tricks an artist can use.

In this painting, Canaletto makes us feel we can look into the far distance, right to the end of the canal. We might be on a boat in the middle of the canal. How does Canaletto do it?

Follow the lines of the roofs and the banks of the canal with your finger. They meet together in the middle like this:

These meeting lines make us see a deep space, which, of course, is not really there at all. In this deep space Canaletto has put the walls of Venetian palaces and churches, the water of the canal, and the clear, warm summer sky of Italy.

In this famous painting by Poussin, the frightened man is running along a path that zigzags around the seated woman and the lake like this:

It is this zigzag line that leads our eyes from the near foreground to the far distance.

J. M. W. Turner (1775–1851)
RAIN, STEAM AND SPEED—
THE GREAT WESTERN RAILWAY
(1844)
91 × 122cm
National Gallery, London

Nicolas Poussin (1594–1665)
LANDSCAPE WITH A MAN
KILLED BY A SNAKE (about 1648)
119 × 199cm
National Gallery, London

This is one of the first great paintings of a railway train. It shows all the excitement and the power and mystery of new machines. Turner has made a window by using a wedge shape like this:

As we look through his window, the train seems to rush straight at us from the far, misty distance.

Edouard Manet (1832–1883)
THE RACES AT LONGCHAMP (1864)
44 × 85cm
Potter Palmer Collection,
Art Institute of Chicago

Look at the pictures on these two pages.

In which of them has the artist used lines that meet together?

a zigzag line?

a wedge shape?

Answers on page 59.

Claude Monet (1840–1926)
THE POPLARS (about 1891)
93 × 74cm
Fitzwilliam Museum, Cambridge

John Constable (1776–1837)
FLATFORD MILL (1816–1817)
102 × 127cm
Tate Gallery, London

Domenico Veneziano (active 1356–1372)
THE ANNUNCIATION
28 × 54cm
Fitzwilliam Museum, Cambridge

Pick up an apple or touch your head. Both feel firm and round, although your face has various odd bits on it such as a nose and ears. Now touch this page. It too is firm, but it is completely flat.

The picture on this page is a self-portrait by Rembrandt; on the opposite page is a painting of three musicians by Picasso. Both are painted on flat canvas, but Rembrandt has made his face, body, and hand seem to be rounded like those of a living person.

He does this with shading to make the picture look as if light is shining in from one side. The parts that face the light are bright, and those away from it are dark and shaded. Look at someone sitting near a bright light and see where light changes to shade on the face, body, and hands. By carefully painting this change from light to shade, Rembrandt makes us see the rounded shapes of his body.

Rembrandt van Rijn (1606–1669)
SELF PORTRAIT (1640)
102 × 80cm
National Gallery, London

Picasso makes us see his three musicians, but his painting has no shading or rounded shapes. You could make a jigsaw by cutting out the different shapes with a pair of scissors. Could you make a jigsaw out of the different shapes in Rembrandt's painting? You would probably find it impossible, because all the shapes and colors blend into each other and the outlines often disappear completely. What instruments are Picasso's musicians playing? Can you find the dog?

Pablo Picasso (1881–1975)
THREE MUSICIANS (1921)
201 × 223cm
Mrs Simon Guggenheim Fund,
Museum of Modern Art, New York

Try some simple experiments for yourself.

Turn a flat shape like this   into a rounded shape

Turn this flat shape   into this

Now draw a big outline of Rembrandt's face from his self portrait and see if you can add the shading to make it look rounded.

This picture was painted about 200 years ago by an English artist, James Seymour. He loved the sports of hunting and racing. You can see in his picture a lot of details that he must have observed in real life. But we are going to look at the way he has made his painting.

James Seymour (1702–1752)
THE KILL AT ASHDOWN PARK
(1743)
181 × 239cm
Tate Gallery, London

What is the biggest object that he has shown? Although he has painted it very small, it is the house, which is large enough to hold hundreds of people and horses. Seymour has painted it so small because it is in the far distance. He has noticed that as things get further away they seem to get smaller and smaller until they vanish completely.

But look again. Do you think he has always got the sizes of near and distant objects right? Hasn't he made a few mistakes? Do you think the horses in the bottom right-hand corner are the correct size? Shouldn't they be bigger, because they are closer than the others? Although the artist has made a few mistakes, it would not be difficult to make a map of this painting and mark where everything is. See if you can make one.

This painting was made over 500 years ago by a Spanish artist called Bernardo Martorell. You would not be able to make an accurate map from it to show precisely where everything is. The distance does not spread out realistically as it does in Seymour's painting. Instead it becomes squashed against the top edge of the picture.

Look at the castle in the background. It looks like a toy castle, and the people inside it are much too large. The horse that St. George rides is much too small for him, and the princess is almost as big as the horse, although she is in the distance. Do you think the sizes have come out all wrong because the artist didn't know what he was doing? Or are there reasons for the sizes?

Martorell has made the people larger than the castle because he wants us to know they are there. St. George is bigger than his horse because he is more important, and Martorell is making sure we notice the fine clothes that the princess is wearing.

Bernardo Martorell (active 1427–1452)
ST. GEORGE AND THE DRAGON
(about 1430)
142 × 97cm
Charles Deering Collection,
The Art Institute of Chicago

An artist often has a difficult choice. Should he paint only what he sees? Or should he paint what he knows is really there, even though it would be impossible to see it in real life?

In which of the pictures on these two pages has the artist

spread distant things out realistically so that you could make a map or plan of them?

squashed distant things against the edge of the picture?

Answers on page 59.

Marc Chagall (1887–)
I AND THE VILLAGE (1911)
191 × 151cm
Mrs Simon Guggenheim Fund,
Museum of Modern Art, New York

Edgar Degas (1834–1917)
THE REHEARSAL OF THE BALLET
ON THE STAGE (1878–79)
53 × 72cm
Havemeyer Collection,
Metropolitan Museum of Art, New York

Benozzo Gozzoli (1420–1497)
ST. PETER AND SIMON MAGUS
40 × 46cm
Metropolitan Museum of Art, New York

Duccio di Buoninsegna (active 1278–1318)
NATIVITY WITH THE PROPHETS
ISAIAH AND EZEKIEL (main panel
only)
44 × 45cm
Andrew W. Mellon Collection,
National Gallery of Art,
Washington, D.C.

When we compare sizes, we have to use our eyes. But we use other parts of our bodies as well: our fingers, hands, or feet. I expect you know your height, but do you know the sizes of other parts of your body? Which is larger, your hand or your face? Put your hand over your face and find out. What is the distance around your wrist? What is the measurement around your neck? Which part of your body is exactly half-way between the top of your head and your toes? Are both your eyes the same size?

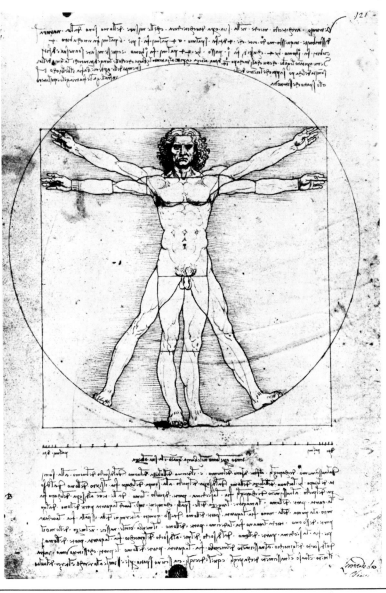

Leonardo da Vinci made the drawing on this page. He knew that all bodies are different, but he had an idea that there was a perfectly shaped body that would fit into a circle and square just as he has drawn. How near do you come to Leonardo's idea of a perfect body? You can find out by measuring, or by drawing a circle and square like his on the floor and seeing if you can fit inside them.

The next three pages show some of the ways in which artists have painted faces and bodies.

Leonardo da Vinci (1452–1519)
PROPORTIONS OF THE HUMAN
FIGURE—VITRUVIAN MAN
(about 1492)
34 × 25cm
Accademia, Venice

Auguste Renoir (1841–1919)
BY THE SEASHORE (1883)
92 × 72cm
Mrs. H. O. Havemeyer Bequest,
Metropolitan Museum of Art, New York

Renoir has not painted this girl exactly as he saw her. He has imagined how a perfect girl would look and has taken away all the faults and blemishes that exist in real life.

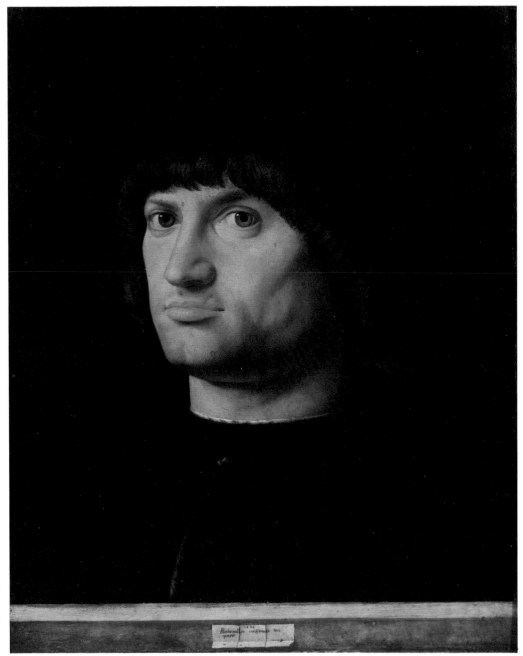

Antonello da Messina (about 1430–1479)
PORTRAIT OF A MAN or
THE SOLDIER OF FORTUNE
(1475)
34 × 28cm
Musée du Louvre, Paris

This man did not have a perfect face, and Antonello da Messina did not pretend that he had. He painted the man exactly as he looked, with all his faults. If you look carefully, you can see a scar on his lip.

Francis Bacon (1909–   )
ISABEL RAWSTHORNE (1966)
81 × 69cm
Tate Gallery, London

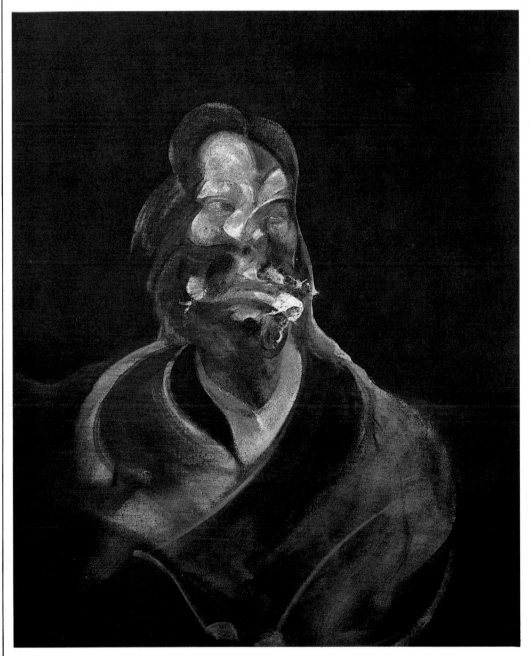

Francis Bacon knows that people don't really look like this. He does not want us to think about perfection or the exact way people look. He wants us to think about what they are feeling.

When you have strong feelings and wishes, they can very often seem to push you about in different directions, rather as in this painting. Artists sometimes distort faces and bodies to make us think about inner feelings that may never show on a person's face or body in real life.

In which of the pictures on these two pages has the artist

painted exactly what he saw?

made a perfect face and body?

shown emotions by painting a distorted face and body?

Answers on page 59.

Chaim Soutine (1894–1943)
THE PASTRY CHEF
Gift of the Joseph H. Hazen Foundation,
National Gallery of Art,
Washington, D.C.

François Boucher (1703–1770)
MADAME DE POMPADOUR
201 × 157cm
Alte Pinakothek, Munich

Henri de Toulouse-Lautrec (1864–1901)
MONSIEUR BOILEAU AT THE
CAFÉ (1893)
80 × 65cm
Hinman B. Hurlburt Collection,
The Cleveland Museum of Art

Francisco Goya (1756–1828)
THE DUKE OF WELLINGTON
(1812–14)
64 × 52cm
National Gallery, London

Madame de Pompadour and the Duke of
Wellington were both real people. If you find
out more about them by reading history books
or biographies, you will be able to judge for
yourself whether or not their portraits give a
good impression of what they were like.

Without light we would not be able to see anything at all. Light comes to us naturally as sunlight and moonlight, or we can make it artificially with candles, electricity, and so on. Different sorts of light alter the way things look, and artists use light in their own special ways.

Jan Vermeer (1632–1675)
YOUNG WOMAN WITH A
WATER JUG
(about 1663)
117 × 104cm
Metropolitan Museum of Art, New York

The Dutch artist Vermeer has taken the greatest care to show how light filters into a room through a half-open window. What time of day do you think Vermeer shows in his painting? Does daylight stay the same or does it change minute by minute? Rare moments of calm and peace like the one in the painting can be very short. Vermeer captured this brief moment almost 300 years ago, but it still exists for us today.

Here the great Italian artist Titian has not tried to imitate the light of the sun. Look at the sky and the shadows. Although it is daylight, there are stars in the sky, and the shadows are not in the right places for sunlight. How has Titian used light?

Titian (Tiziano Vecellio, about 1480–1576)
BACCHUS AND ARIADNE (1523)
175 × 191cm
National Gallery, London

It looks as if he has made spotlights shine on things he wants us to see clearly and used shadows to hide anything that is not so important. The light in his picture is more like that of a stage or film set than of real life.

André Derain (1880–1954)
POOL OF LONDON (1906)
66 × 99cm
Tate Gallery, London

This painting is not like a stage set or the real world. Derain has completely changed the colors. He has made the sky green and the buildings blue. Has he changed all the colors, or has he left some things colored naturally?

Derain has invented his own special light. He has changed the colors to make the picture full of blues and reds and greens, which clash together and jump about in a lively way, rather like the atmosphere in a busy port.

In which of the pictures on pages 35 and 36 has the artist used

natural light?

artificial light?

a spotlight?

his own special light?

Answers on page 59.

Aelbert Cuyp (1620–1691)
A HILLY RIVER LANDSCAPE
(about 1655–66)
135 × 200cm
National Gallery, London

Paul Delaroche (1795–1856)
THE EXECUTION OF LADY JANE
GREY (1833)
246 × 297cm
National Gallery, London

Georges Seurat (1859–1891)
INVITATION TO THE SIDESHOW
(1887)
100 × 150cm
Stephen C. Clark Bequest,
Metropolitan Museum of Art, New York

Karl Schmidt-Rottluf (1884–1976)
LOFTHUS—1911
87 × 96cm
Kunsthalle, Hamburg

Look very carefully at this painting by Velasquez. Make a list of the colors that the artist has used. Start at the top of your list with the colors that appear most and work down to those that appear least. Look again and see which colors the artist has used to show the brightest light and the darkest shadow.

Diego Rodriguez de Silva Velasquez
(1599–1660)
THE WATER-SELLER OF SEVILLE
105 × 81cm
(about 1620)
Wellington Museum, Apsley House,
London

Does your list show that Velasquez has used nearly all browns and blacks and dark colors? You will see that he has used white for bright light and black or grey for shadows. Velasquez's colors make us concentrate on the surfaces, shapes, and textures, and on the exact place where light catches them. Look how carefully he has painted the glass, showing precisely where the light falls.

Now make a list of colors in this painting by Monet. It will show blue, red, orange, yellow—clear, bright rainbow colors. Monet has not used browns or blacks. Notice how he has used yellow for bright light and blue or violet for the shadows.

Claude Monet (1840–1926)
THE HOUSES OF PARLIAMENT, WESTMINSTER (1904)
81 × 92cm
Jeu de Paume, Musée du Louvre, Paris

Monet's painting glows as if it were a rainbow, but it is not possible to tell the shape and texture of objects or the exact place where the light is falling.

Even the whitest light is made up of bright colors; a rainbow allows us to see them separately. When sunlight shines through raindrops, it is broken up into a series of bright colors. If you use a triangular wedge of glass called a prism to break up a ray of light, you will get the same six colors, always in the same order:

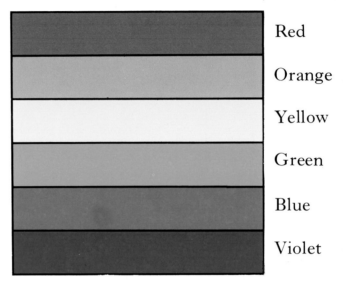

Red

Orange

Yellow

Green

Blue

Violet

We call them the spectrum. You can sometimes see a spectrum when a beam of light catches a piece of cut or broken glass.

Now compare the colors in my diagram with your list of colors in Monet's painting. They should be almost the same. Monet understood that light is composed of different colors, so instead of using just white paint for bright sunlight, he used all the colors he knew were really there.

When the sun is shining, look carefully at the shadows. What color are they? Are they black or blue? Aren't some shadows red or green? What is the color of a sparkle of sunlight? Can you always tell exactly where light and shadow are? Can you always see the outlines of things or does sunlight sometimes make them dissolve and disappear, as in Monet's painting?

I am not going to show you any paintings on the next three pages. Instead, here are some experiments you can do with paints. Try painting the spectrum, but make sure you get the colors absolutely right.

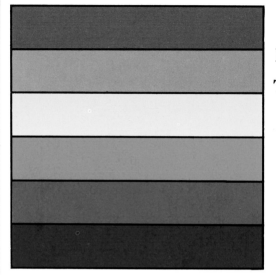

Now see what happens if you add white to your colors. They become light and clear.

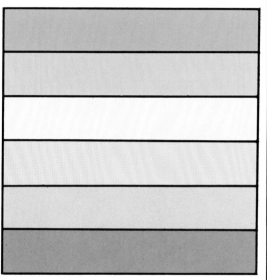

If you add black,

the colors become rich and

dark.

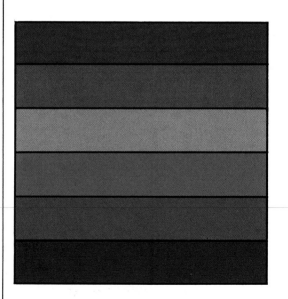

If you add grey,

the colors lose

their brightness.

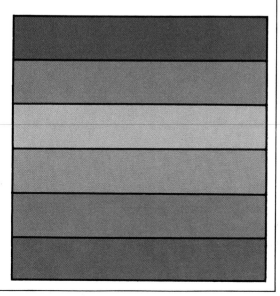

Three colors from the spectrum cannot be made from other colors. They are called primary colors.

We can use them to make other colors in the spectrum:

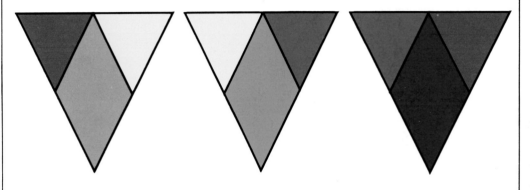

Some colors clash and vibrate together. Here are the strongest color clashes you can paint. We call these pairs complementary colors:

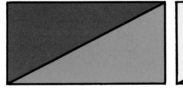  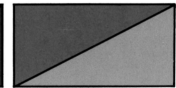

Some colors blend together and do not clash:

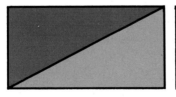 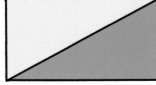 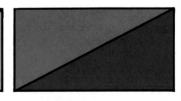

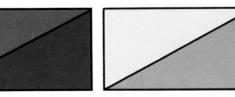 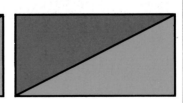

Look hard at these blue shapes:

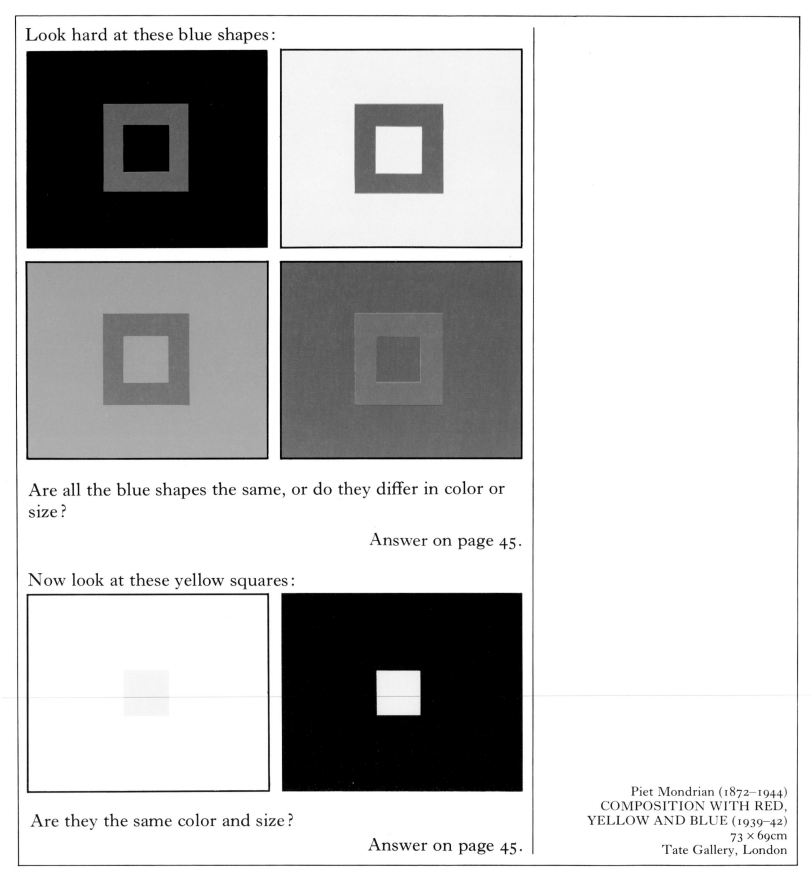

Are all the blue shapes the same, or do they differ in color or size?

Answer on page 45.

Now look at these yellow squares:

Are they the same color and size?

Answer on page 45.

Piet Mondrian (1872–1944)
COMPOSITION WITH RED,
YELLOW AND BLUE (1939–42)
73 × 69cm
Tate Gallery, London

Look at the coloring of the pictures on this page and the next two pages. In which has the artist used

colors that mainly fight each other?

colors that mainly blend together?

almost no color at all?

primary colors?

In which has the artist experimented with the shapes and sizes of colors?

Answers on page 59.

James McNeil Whistler (1834–1903)
THE WHITE GIRL—SYMPHONY
IN WHITE, No. 1 (1862)
214 × 108cm
Harris Whittemore Collection
National Gallery of Art,
Washington, D.C.

Frank Stella (1936–   )
TUFTONBORO IV (1966)
254 × 276cm
Gift of David Whitney,
Museum of Modern Art, New York

Georges Braque (1882–1963)
STILL LIFE. THE TABLE (1928)
81 × 131cm
Chester Dale Collection
National Gallery of Art,
Washington, D.C.

Morris Louis (1912–1962)
THIRD ELEMENTS
218 × 130cm
From the Blanchette Rockefeller Fund,
Museum of Modern Art, New York

Answers to questions on page 42.
The blue and yellow shapes are
always the same. It is the colors
next to them that make them look
different.

Look carefully at the pictures on these two pages. Are they cheerful or gloomy pictures? You have probably noticed that some paintings can make us feel cheerful while others can make us feel sad, or peaceful, or even angry, just as pieces of music can make us have different moods and feelings.

Hogarth's portrait of the Graham children is a large picture. I hope you agree it is a cheerful one. He certainly meant it to be cheerful except for one small detail. Can you see what the detail is?

Look at the colors he uses: they are dark and rather gloomy. Not very cheerful at all. But look at the things in the picture and at what the children are doing. They are all smiling. The boy is playing a musical box, and one girl is dancing. The baby is holding a biscuit and reaching for some cherries. Hogarth makes his picture cheerful by filling it with happy children and good things like delicious fruit and beautiful clothes.

Did you notice the detail of the cat stalking the caged bird? They are easy to miss, but Hogarth puts them there to remind us that cruelty and fear still exist alongside happiness.

Van Gogh's painting does not have any smiling faces or good things to eat or games to play. It is a rather simple picture of a simple bedroom. We don't usually think of chairs and tables and beds as smiling or happy, but Van Gogh's picture is a cheerful one. How does he give this feeling?

Vincent van Gogh (1853–1890)
BEDROOM AT ARLES (1889)
73 × 92cm
National Museum Vincent van Gogh,
Amsterdam

He does it by filling his picture with warm and cheerful colors: the yellow of sunlight and the blue of a cloudless sky. We know from Van Gogh's letters that the chairs and the bed were made of white wood and were not yellow at all. He changed their colors in his painting so that we would think of sunlight and happiness.

Can you detect something odd about this painting? Look at the floor for a clue.

Although the picture seems to be full of bright sunlight, there are no shadows.

Can you make a list of colors that are happy and cheerful? Make another list of sad colors. Think about your lists as you look at the pictures on the next two pages.

Look at the pictures on these two pages. Could you describe in words the mood or feeling that each picture gives you?

Henri Rousseau (1844–1910)
TROPICAL STORM WITH TIGER
(1891)
130 × 162cm
National Gallery, London

48

In which pictures does the
artist express his feelings by
painting mainly things,
people or animals?

In which paintings does he
use only color?

In which does he use color
with things, people or
animals?

Answers on page 59.

Henri Matisse (1869–1954)
DANCE (1909)
261 × 390cm
Gift of Nelson A. Rockefeller in honour of
Alfred H. Barr, Jr.,
Museum of Modern Art, New York

Mark Rothko (1903–1970)
LIGHT RED OVER BLACK (1957)
233 × 153cm
Tate Gallery, London

Salvador Dali (1904–   )
THE PERSISTENCE OF MEMORY
(1931)
24 × 33cm
Museum of Modern Art, New York

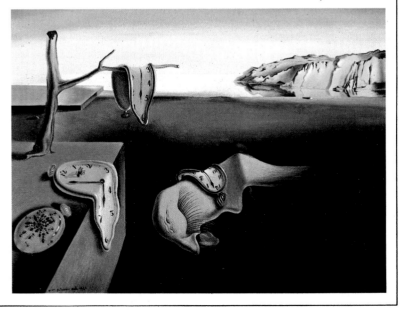

Two of the next four paintings are calm and still, and two are full of energy and movement. Which are they? In each picture the artist has used a pattern or shape to convey a feeling. Can you work out what the patterns and shapes are, and how they are used?

Claude Lorrain (1600–1682)
LANDSCAPE: AENEAS AT DELOS
(1672)
100 × 134cm
National Gallery, London

Claude's painting shows a peaceful moment of the day. He has used soft colors that blend together. The people are standing very calmly, and there is not a breath of wind. Run your finger down the sides of the building and then across the edge of the water and the horizon. Claude has carefully composed his picture with straight horizontal and vertical lines like this:

and this pattern creates a feeling of calm and stillness.

Matisse's painting is full of energy. He has used large areas of bright color that clash together and fight each other. He hasn't used a pattern of horizontal or vertical lines. Can you find another pattern? If you look carefully, you will see that the colored areas form this lively spiral:

Henri Matisse (1869–1954)
THE SNAIL (1953)
286 × 287cm
Tate Gallery, London

Now you can see why he has called his picture "The Snail".

Rubens's picture is filled with the energy of great armies fighting together. Has he used bright colors that fight together? Or has he used some other idea? Look at the soldiers and the horses. They don't all fit snugly in the picture; some are rushing in at the edge and others seem about to leap out. Rubens makes his painting seem too small to show all the movement and details of the fierce battle. The shapes rush out of the picture to give a sensation of power and energy.

Peter Paul Rubens (1577–1640)
BATTLE OF THE AMAZONS
(before 1619)
121 × 166cm
Alte Pinakothek, Munich

Raphael's picture is very peaceful. He has used soft colors and painted as perfectly as he can. He makes our eyes move very calmly and steadily up toward the top of the painting, as though we were looking up to heaven. You will see that Raphael has arranged the figures in the shape of a triangle, like this:

It is an important shape. The triangle rests firmly and securely on the ground and at the same time points steadily upward.

Raphael (Raffaelo Sanzio, 1483–1520)
MADONNA AND CHILD
or LA BELLE JARDINIÈRE (1507)
122 × 80cm
Musée du Louvre, Paris

Look at the pictures on these three pages. In which of them have the artists used

horizontal and vertical lines?

a spiral?

a triangle?

or made the picture burst out of the frame?

Answers on page 59.

Caspar David Friedrich (1774–1840)
THE WANDERER/
OVER THE SEA OF MIST
(about 1818)
95 × 75cm
Kunsthalle, Hamburg

Gino Severini (1883–1966)
SUBURBAN TRAIN ARRIVING
IN PARIS (1915)
87 × 116cm
Tate Gallery, London

J. M. W. Turner (1775–1851)
THE SHIPWRECK (1805)
171 × 242cm
Tate Gallery, London

Artists, as we have seen, have many ways of making pictures, but we should also realize that they paint for many reasons. Sometimes to give pleasure or show unexpected things. Sometimes to make us imagine things we cannot see with our eyes or to make us share their dreams. Sometimes to make us think about the difficult or unpleasant side of life, which we may try to ignore. Sometimes to make us think about ourselves and who we are. Sometimes just for the sake of showing the way pictures are made and how an artist uses things like colors, paint, or brush strokes.

George Stubbs (1724–1806)
REAPERS (1785)
90 × 137cm
Tate Gallery, London

Finally, let me show you how some of the great artists saw themselves. Study their faces and see if you can guess which of them painted the pictures that you have seen in this book. Look back through the book to find if you are right, and as you do so, remember what all great artists know: once you start to look and think and imagine, there is no reason ever to stop.

1

3

5

2

4

6

7

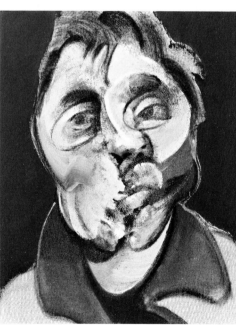

8

9

10

1
Leonardo da Vinci (1452–1519)
SELF PORTRAIT (about 1512)
33 × 21cm
Royal Library, Turin

2
Peter Paul Rubens (1577–1640)
SELF PORTRAIT WITH ISABELLA
BRANDT (1609–10)
178 × 136cm
Alte Pinakothek, Munich

3
William Hogarth (1697–1764)
SELF PORTRAIT WITH PUG (1745)
90 × 70cm
Tate Gallery, London

4
Francisco Goya (1746–1828)
SELF PORTRAIT (1799)
215 × 150cm
British Museum

5
J. M. W. Turner (1775–1851)
SELF PORTRAIT (about 1798)
74 × 58cm
Tate Gallery, London

6
Caspar David Friedrich (1774–1840)
SELF PORTRAIT (1802)
18 × 11cm
Kunsthalle, Hamburg

7
Paul Cézanne (1839–1906)
SELF PORTRAIT (about 1880)
34 × 26cm
National Gallery, London

8
Henri Rousseau (1844–1910)
MYSELF, PORTRAIT–LANDSCAPE
146 × 114cm
Narodni Gallery, Prague

9
Vincent van Gogh (1853–1890)
SELF PORTRAIT WITH GREY HAT
(1887)
44 × 38cm
National Museum Vincent van Gogh,
Amsterdam

10
Francis Bacon (1909–   )
SELF PORTRAIT (1969)
36 × 31cm
Marlborough Fine Art, London

Answers

Page

12   *February* 118 × 163cm

13   *Piano* 183 × 277 × 114cm
Zero through Nine 137 × 105cm

14   *Mr and Mrs Andrews* is like a window
Soft Drainpipe comes out of the wall

15   *The Marriage of Arnolfini* is like a window
Picture with Light Centre is like the palm of your hand

18   *The Races at Longchamp* uses a wedge shape
The Poplars uses a zigzag line

19   *Flatford Mill* uses zigzag lines
The Annunciation uses lines that meet together

24   *I and the Village* squashes distant things against the edge of the picture
The Rehearsal of the Ballet on the Stage spreads distant things out realistically

25   *St Peter and Simon Magus* spreads distant things out realistically
Nativity squashes distant things against the edge of the picture

30   *The Pastry Chef* shows emotions through a distorted face and body
Madame de Pompadour shows a perfect face and body

31   *Monsieur Boileau at the Café* and *The Duke of Wellington* both show what the artist saw

35   *A Hilly River Landscape* uses natural light
The Execution of Lady Jane Grey uses a spotlight

36   *Invitation to the Sideshow* uses artificial light
Lofthus uses the artist's own special light

43   *Composition with Red, Yellow and Blue* uses primary colors
The White Girl uses almost no color at all

44   *Tuftonboro IV* experiments with the shapes and sizes of colors
Still Life, The Table uses colors that mainly blend together

45   *Third Elements* uses colors that mainly fight each other

48   *Tropical Storm with Tiger* uses color, things and an animal to express feelings

49   *Dance* uses mainly people to express the artist's feelings
Light Red over Black uses only color
The Persistence of Memory uses color and things

54   *The Wanderer* uses a triangle

55   *Suburban Train Arriving in Paris* is bursting out of its frame
The Shipwreck uses a spiral

56   *Reapers* uses horizontal and vertical lines

Galleries

Artists